D1595663

THE
BUCKS
CAMP LOG
1916–1928

A WISCONSIN DEER CAMP DIARY

THE
BUCKS
CAMP LOG
1916–1928

A WISCONSIN DEER CAMP DIARY

Willow Creek Press

© 2006 Marjorie Williams

Published by Willow Creek Press
P.O. Box 147, Minocqua, Wisconsin 54548

Illustrations © Dave Wollangk

ISBN 13: 978-1-59543-438-8

First published in 1974 by Wisconsin Sportsman Publications. Minor grammatical changes have been made to the original hand-written journal entries unless otherwise noted in the text.

Printed in the United States

"Now go to the hills and bubbling spring,
Listen to the voice of the wolf dog ring,
To beavers splash and the snort of deer,
Commune with cosmos and the gods of cheer."

TABLE OF CONTENTS

PREFACE

ometime around 1916 a group of men from Ladysmith, Wisconsin, banded together and formed what was referred to as Bucks Club. These men loved to hunt, and took great pride in their skills of woodsmanship. They acquired an old log building that had formerly been part of a lumber camp. It was located in the Blue Hills of northern Rusk County where even today there is much scenic and unspoiled territory. Every November, when the hunting fever began stirring in their blood, the members headed for the hills. Doctors, lawyers, dentists, bankers, ministers (to identify just a few) dropped everything and left for the woods to hunt deer.

As a youngster I was always greatly mystified and awed by this November ritual of deer hunting and the inevitable exodus to Bucks Camp. Several weeks before the event took place, my father began to acquire a kind of glow, and the smell of gun oil and rubber boots hung in the air. An object referred to as a pack sac was brought forth and filled with wool socks, flannel shirts, and more to the point, I thought, a big bar of German sweet chocolate for quick energy in case he got lost in the woods.

I knew what happened on the home front while the men were off on this hunting foray. My mother locked more doors than usual; we got to sleep later and all the neighborhood women and children gathered for a manless Thanksgiving dinner.

But where, I wondered, was this famous Buck Camp that the men headed for and what sort of earth shaking things did they do when they got there?

Many years later these questions were answered when I came across a frayed black ledger book entitled *The Bucks Log.* One of the men must have started keeping a record the first year they were there in 1916, and the Log was then left there from year to year. By the time I had finished reading the tattered black ledger book, I understood much better what Bucks Camp was all about, and I think I know why my father returned from the hunting season bewhiskered and tired, but supremely happy as he hung his deer in the garage for all to admire. I know better too why the next November the whole process started over again. *The Bucks Log* reveals it all.

Marjorie Williams

1917

Although Bucks Camp was originated in 1916, it was not until the 1917 season that the Bucks Camp Log was started in earnest. The very first entry records a startling incident involving D.L. Tainter, a recluse living near the camp. A local newspaper of that era described Tainter as "a strange, quaint character, one of the fading battalion of that old regime of hunters, trappers and woodsmen whose names are so indelibly written in the history and romance of Wisconsin. Tainter was an atheist. At one time he was said to have been deeply religious and some years past he would read his Bible for a time and then cry out, 'It's all a damned lie!' and tear the leaves from the Bible and scatter them about. He insisted that no preacher act at his funeral. 'If one does,' the hermit said, 'I'll get right up in my coffin and curse him.'

Despite his eccentricities, or perhaps because of them, Tainter was considered an endeared friend of the Bucks. Numerous references in the log point this out. But let the Bucks tell it...

November 20th, 1917

Arrivals in camp:

L.C. Streater, L.E. McGill, H.F. Davis, Glenn H. Williams, E.W. Day, H.M. Munroe, F.E. Munroe, N.J. Smith, H.W. True, Elmer

W. Hill, J.W. Carow, W.F. O'Connor and E.W. Hill, Sr. Visitor, Rev. Mielecki, Minister of Kelner, Wis. and a guest of H.M. Munroe.

Herman Le Blanc, the chef, and G.W. Heaverin arrived yesterday and opened up the camp. We found everything in good order with a supply of wood cut an hauled up to camp.

Carow and Streater returned from Tainter's place and reported that they found him dead in his bed from a gunshot wound in the head.

Weather warm and pleasant. No frost in the ground.

November 21st, 1917

Cloudy and rain showers.

Word having been received of the death of D.L. Tainter, the entire membership of the Bucks Club went over in the morning and arrived at the Tainter residence in the forenoon.

We found Mr. Tainter dead in his bed. He had been shot through the mouth, the bullet passing up through his head causing instantaneous death. His rifle lay on the floor beside the bed with an empty shell in the barrel. His dog had been shot and killed and was found lying in front of the kennel. An empty shell from Tainter's gun was found nearby.

The evidence pointed so strongly to suicide that an inquest was deemed unnecessary. A neighbor arrived with a team and casket and we placed the body in it. After a short prayer by Rev. Mielecki, Mr. Tainter was taken to Birchwood for burial.

The club then returned to camp somewhat sobered.

November 22nd, 1917

Cloudy and colder with high winds.

Rev. Mielecki, G.H. Munroe, E.W. Day and J.W. Carow all reported that they had each hung up a deer.

G.H. Williams had shot at a wolf.

J.W. Carow and Doc Day have invented a sound box for the Victrola to take the place of the one that was lost. We now have music.

Carow's "medicine chest" was drawn upon for colds and minor ailments.

The smear game offered much amusement for several.

E.W. Hill, Sr. is on the sick list with an apparent attack of grippe.

Lake partly frozen.

No beaver in the lake this year.

November 23rd, 1917

Deer scarce. Hills higher than ever before. All hands report in tired.

H.W. True only one to kill a deer.

G.H. Williams was chased several miles by a fox.

Henry Davis was lost for hours in the woods and explained by saying, "I was just following my nose."

Dr. O'Connor shot six times at a deer without making a hit and then tried to catch it. He isn't feeling well tonight, but won't admit that the deer was the cause.

F.E. Munroe's one hair needs curling.

Rev. Mielecki has neither taken a drink nor sworn today.

J.W. Carow has been telling ghost stories.

L.E. McGill is so ornery tonight that he would not come in for dinner. He built a fire in the swamp southeast of the north end of High Bridge and pretended to eat just the same.

> There was a scribe named McGill
> He threw a terrible quill
> He would tan your hide
> Or give you a ride
> And all you could do was keep still.
> *   *   *   *   *
> There was a man named Munroe
> He'd rather shoot a buck than a doe
> He jumped on a log
> But not being a frog
> He the brush with his bullets did mow.
> *   *   *   *   *
> There was a man named Streater
> With Smith he went out to greet her
> Smith said, "Which one?"
> He said, "Oh, let her run
> "When she is far enough our bullets will meet her."

November 24th, 1917

It has been misty all day with a west wind. The lake froze over last night, but it is not safe yet.

No deer killed today. Munroe and Carow had shooting at a big buck. They wounded but lost him.

McGill and Doc Day hunted in the Lone Pine Country. It was so misty that they hunted hand in hand. They say they only hunted a half mile all day because upon hitting a tree they did not dare let go hands, and could not agree on which direction to take.

Streater and Davis killed a rabbit for luck. Each took one of the hind feet. When one of them kills a buck they will know which is the lucky one.

E.W. Hill, Sr. is feeling better.

Irwin True arrived in camp today.

Dr. O'Connor went up towards the High Bridge Green where he could get enough distance for his gun. He says his gun shoots with such velocity that if he hits a deer nearer than 100 rods the bullet goes through him so fast he doesn't even feel it.

> Smith is a man of his worth
> He was born on the day of his birth
> He was married as they say
> On his own wedding day
> And will die on his last day on earth.
> *　　*　　*　　*　　*
> True who came with a Tin Liz
> Affirms that life is what it is
> For he early had learnt
> If life were what it weren't
> It would not be that which it is.

Hill, Sr. is so good and wise
In fact an angel in disguise
With a heart so big
That the ham of a pig
Gives you know idea of its size.
*   *   *   *   *
There's a Le Blanc from Quebec
Who fell in the lake to his neck
When we asked, "Are you friz?"
He replied, "Yes I is,
"But we don't call this cold in Quebec."
*   *   *   *   *
Elmer Hill did dare
To smile as he rode on a bear
They came back from the ride
With Elmer inside
And the smile on the face of the bear.
*   *   *   *   *
There's Hill with the hairy chin
Who is so exceedingly thin
That when he essayed
to sip lemonade
He slipped through the straw and fell in.

November 25th, 1917

Cloudy with a west wind all day. No snow yet.

F. Munroe, Elmer Hill and Carow made a drive through the Hardwood south of the lakes. Drove out one deer but it went back in again before the watchers could shoot.

Streater and Doc Day went over toward the Polish settlement. They met Zolubak who reported that Mr. Tainter's brother from Menomonie had come in to hunt with Tainter not knowing he was dead. He ordered Zolubak not to fill the grave at Birchwood as he intended to move the body. He says he is going to have the law on Bucks Club for not holding an inquest, for not getting a permit to bury the body, etc. etc. He has gone back to consult his lawyer.

The bunch drove the vicinity of the Poise stump this afternoon. Mr. E.W. Hill, Sr. was feeling well enough to join the bunch. A lead mine could be started with the bullets we left down there. We had five deer surrounded. The bombardment sounded like an English barrage. Deer were running everywhere. They were so thick around Mr. Hill, Sr. that he had to push them away beyond the end of his gun so he could shoot them. He got buck fever so bad that he was shooting in a circle. Mr. True said the air was so thick around Mr. Hill, Sr. that he could not shoot through it.

McGill got lost from Doc Day. He built his fire for dinner just over the hill from camp, not having recognized his location. He then saw the lake and camp and made his way in. When he saw

Doc sitting on the edge of his bunk smoking his pipe, he burst out, "What the hell are you doing here?"

The joke being on McGill, they made him go out and cut some wood. That was a terrible punishment for Mac.

Mr. Hill, Sr. has been entertaining us tonight with stories about old logging days. At intervals he stops to tell again how he got buck fever this afternoon. He is now telling it for the sixteenth time. He is pleased and disappointed by spells over the recollection of it. Here goes the seventeenth time.

Now Frank is explaining how his last shot may have hit a deer. Each now thinks he hit one. Now they are wondering if they ought to go out there with a rake and see how many dead deer they can find.

> There's Frank Munroe with his beard
> Who said, "It is just as I feared,
> A porky pig
> And a woodchuck big
> Have both made nests in my beard."
>
> *   *   *   *   *
>
> There's McGill and Davis so bold and blunt
> When you mention their noses, they only grunt,
> "Our bills we don't mind them
> For we are behind them
> But we pity you fellows in front."

*   *   *   *   *

There was a young man named Carow
Who thought to kill deer with bow and arrow
Then he shot at two
With his little twenty-two
But all he got was a poor little sparrow.

November 26th, 1917

Still cloudy and no snow. East and southeast wind. It is snowing
tonight.

Doc Day went home today.

We know now that Mr. Hill, Sr. hit one of those deer yesterday. It crossed the right-of-way bleeding. We followed it today over William's Hill, but lost the trail.

Neither Steater nor Davis got a deer, so we still do not know which rabbit foot is the lucky one.

November 27th, 1917

Cloudy all day. Southeast wind.

There was tracking snow this morning, and everybody sallied forth sure he would get a buck.

Streater's rabbit foot was certainly working. Mr. True and Irwin, Streater and Carow went up north west of the High Bridge Green. Streater was standing on a stump while Carow was stumping out a pot hole. Mr. True and Irwin were quite a ways west.

Suddenly over a hill came a buck. The second shot Streater got him through the heart. He marked him down until Carow could get to him, when suddenly here comes another buck, bigger than the first one, straight at Streater. In self defense Streater had to civilize this one too with another bullet through the heart.

There was a procession into camp with Streater marching ahead with proud step and head up. As he passed, the Bucks doffed their hats and salaamed.

There have been deer all around camp today. Two walked across the lake at about 11 A.M. We have been going miles away to hunt, but the snow showed us that the deer are as numerous close to camp as elsewhere. Tracks of foxes, wolves, wild cats, bears, weasels and minks have also been seen today.

N.J. Went out with McGill to hunt the Lone Pine Country. He got separated from Mac and ended up way off southeast of the Lone Pine Hill at the big beaver dam. He was not lost, but had strayed a long way off. He was a pleased man when Mac finally located him. He was game, though, and coming straight toward camp. Any man ought to be examined who tries to hunt the Lone Pine Country (and this includes Mac).

Mr. Heaverin brought his team in today to take out a load of deer. He is hard at it now trying to beat the boys at smear.

He did.

Heaverin is a man who dotes on smear
He tackles the Bucks without fear
With a Jack and an Ace
And a wry sober face
He cleans the Bucks up every year.

Heaverin is not brave though when ghosts are around
When he put up his horses he heard the sound
Of old Tainter play
On his Fiddle gay
When Heaverin trembled, he shook the ground.

November 28th, 1917

Cloudy. Southeast wind. Very foggy with white frost on the trees and bushes.

Herm at last saw a rabbit and shot it. He wants the fact recorded.

Heaverin took out nine deer.

Most of the boys left camp today.

> Herm usually sees so many deer,
> He claims to have the habit.
> We told him to can the luck
> Or he certainly would crab it.
> So this year
> He saw no deer
> And all he could get was a rabbit.

November 29th, 1917

This poem marks the final entry of the Bucks 1917 deer hunting season. Judging by the scribbled handwriting which appears in the original log, and the obvious lack of their usual unique rhythm, the reader can easily imagine that a generous amount of spirits were imbibed on this day.

The game of smear is quite a game
Sometimes you win and sometimes you lose
As for me I have a lot of same
My judgement's poor
But all the same
I sometimes bid four.

1918

July 23rd, 1918

Elmer Hill and G.H. Williams in from 3:30 to 6 P.M. Found box had been broken open with axe. Skunk had gnawed hole thru floor in corner of kitchen. Skylight broken and open. Nailed tar paper over skylight, tin over hole in floor.

September 22nd, 1918

F.E. Monroe, H.A. Dimock and J.W. Carow arrived in camp at 7 P.M. Drove over in Dimock's Dodge leaving Ladysmith at 4:10 P.M. Left car at Little Wiergor. The camp nearly obscured by weeds. We cut the weeds and burned them and cleaned up camp inside and out. Someone had stolen the oil so Dimock made a dip with some neetsfoot oil and a wick in the top of a can. It worked fine. Frank fixed the box. We hope it will retard the thieves a while.

Went over to the cranberry marsh and picked 2 qts. of berries. In the evening we went over near the old camp and caught six large bullheads. While we were fishing a porky kept squealing off in the woods. We hope he got what he wanted (whatever it was).

November 20th, 1918

The Buck bunch is back in camp ready for the opening of the season tomorrow. Herm Le Blanc and his brother Alex came into camp yesterday and got things into fine shape. The piles of wood that greeted our eyes when we limped in were certainly appreciated.

The following are in camp:

L.C. Streater, G.H. Williams, L.E. McGill, H.W. True, N.J. Smith, Hank Davis, Elmer Hill, Dr. O'Connor, Doc Day, J.W. Carow, F.E. Munroe, H.A. Dimock and O.J. Falge.

Since last year our oldest and well beloved member died—E.W. Hill, Sr. He told us last year it was his last, but we little thought he told us truly. We will miss him very much.

We heard shooting all around today. None of the Bucks broke the law. There are more campers north of us than ever before. The boys counted over 20 camps. Below us there are not so many.

We have a new member with us: district attorney O.J. Falge. He says the lake water is colder than he thought it would be. He had the nerve to ask one of the old Bucks to trade bunks with him, not knowing the tenderfoot bunk is for him alone until he graduates.

> Falge is the boy with nerves to spare,
> You duck him in the lake and he turns not a hair.
> Up he comes with a smile,
> And his face shows no guile.
> He sure is an old timer for all he seems to care.

You should see Doc Day's red pants. With red pants, green coat and a yellow hat someone will take him for a rare flower.

Doc O'Connor with his usual assurance produced what he called a "home made ax." Cost him a dollar! It was made out of a piece of stove pipe and a piece of popple for a handle. Mac said he should fit in a new handle and then put in a new bit and make a good ax out of it.

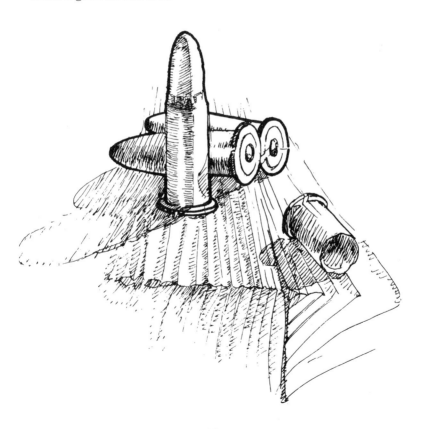

November 21st, 1918

Weather cloudy with north wind. Spit snow all morning.

Carow got a buck at 9 A.M. west of High Bridge Green.

Falge got lost. He started in on the Lone Pine Country and wandered around over to the Twin Greens. Then he followed the creek to the lake and finally followed the shoreline to camp. His pedometer marked off fifteen miles.

Doc Day and Smith wanted a nice little walk, and so were directed to follow the ridge running west from our green to north of the second lake and then north to the Big Ravine. When they finally got there, Smith was said to have mumbled a few naughty words.

> There was a hunter named Smith
> Who said, "That trail of Carow's is a myth,
> It is certainly hard
> And no boulevard
> And I have nothing to rhyme with Smith."

Weather continued windy and cloudy, but it softened up a bit. True killed a duck in the flowage. No more deer killed this afternoon.

November 22nd, 1918

Light snow. Not heavy enough for good tracking.

"Chickadee" O'Connor stayed in camp all morning. Went out

for about fifteen minutes in High Bridge Green, but some La Crosse hunters scared him out.

Surveyor True and chain man Williams have figured out all section corners and are about to locate section corner on range line in Spruce Swamp west of camp.

Streater and Carow pulled the latter's buck to the right-of-way. It weighed 500 lbs. before we gut it out and got it in.

Tonight it is clear and we expect the lake to freeze over.

Hank Davis celebrates his fifty-eighth birthday tonight by filling up on baked beans and prune pie.

No more deer killed today.

November 23rd, 1918

Weather clear and cold. The lake froze over during the night. The trees were so frosty in the morning that it was impossible to see any distance.

No deer were killed and but very few seen.

Our tenderfoot, Falge, saw deer both in morning and afternoon but failed to connect. He insists that the fault is not with the gun. He certainly can find deer.

Mr. True went over to Tainter's. He is the first Buck to make a visit here since the fire last spring. He found the house and barn burned clean—also the dam. The camp buildings were intact and locked up with a "Keep Out" sign tacked to the door. He says there is no personal property left except the boat.

Carow killed a weasel and Mr. True skinned and stitched it to a form.

November 24th, 1918

The day was clear and cold with south and southwest winds.

Elmer got a buck in the swamp which lies east of High Bridge Green. The buck was trotting east and Elmer took a long shot, hitting him in the head. Williams and Carow went out with Elmer after dinner and hauled it in. It is a twin of Carow's.

Mac got a doe in the Lone Pine Country about eight miles away. He hung her up on the side of the cliff. Mac then trailed through a swamp to get back to camp.

We plan to relay the doe in and hope to have it here by next Thanksgiving. You remember what was said last year about men who hunt in Lone Pine Country?

Saw two partridges just outside of camp today, and approached them close enough to take a picture of one of them. It posed perfectly less than ten feet away. An attempt was then made to photograph the other one on the fly.

At target practice today with a .22 revolver, six inch barrel, Mr. True at 50 feet put six bullets out of six into the end of a four inch can.

No cards were played tonight.

November 25th, 1918

Early hunters back to camp today found W.E. Thompson dressed in fancy striped trousers, starched shirt, necktie, etc. Ultimatum issued that the shirt must come off or Thompson takes a duck in the lake through the ice.

Nothing doing in the hunting business, but big doings around the camp dinner table. La Blanc had prepared some of his famous pea soup.

Mr. True came in about dark looking rather mysterious. We had heard two shots from a .32 special in his direction earlier, but could get nothing out of him. Later he produced a mushroomed bullet and put it on the window sill. Turns out that he has killed the biggest buck yet. He got him northeast of the High Bridge.

Everyone swears to get some shooting tomorrow.

> There is a new hunter alert
> Who comes into camp with starch shirt
> But say the boys
> Without much noise
> Off with the shirt
> Or into the lake with a spurt

November 26th, 1918

Doc O'Connor got a buck at the head of the big ravine. Davis says it is hung up about one and a half miles south of Superior. There is no living with Doc now. He certainly is a cocky Irishman. The distance from where he was shooting was 63 rods and he hit the buck in the right eye!!

> O'Connor is the expert guy
> He takes them standing I cannot lie
> He slaps a cripple on the rump
> And makes him jump
> Then hits him in the opposite eye

Mr. True saw two wolves this afternoon.

Doc O'Connor is telling again how, why and where he killed his buck. He stretches the distance each time. Davis who was with him,

just turned around and said, "Hell, Doc, don't stretch that out any longer. I've lost all chance of heaven now trying to back you up!"

I must record the quarrel between Streater and Davis last night after lights were out. They occupy adjoining bunks. The argument was over the question as to which one snores the loudest. Streater said that certainly no one can hear him when Davis is snoring.

Davis said his snore was only Streater's echo. Streater could not see how Davis could snore anyway. He said that the sound would be deadened before it got out of his nose. Davis replied that he snored to keep his nose warm—that snoring pumped hot air into it. Streater then opined that he ought to be able to keep it warm with his hand—at least as far as it could reach.

O'Connor is now warning everyone to stay out of the Lone Pine Country (including Mac), as he is going down there tomorrow to get himself another buck. Cocky Irishman.

November 27th, 1918

The weather is beautiful today. Sunshine and very little wind. Frost diamonds cover the ground and bushes and sparkle in the sunshine showing all the colors of the rainbow.

> Henry Davis is like a pel-i-can
> Few stomachs will hold what his bel-i-can
> He will destroy with his beak
> Enough grub for a week
> But I don't see how the hel-i-can
> *   *   *   *   *
> "Oh, I am a crack shot," says Carow
> At sixty yards I can hit a sparrow
> "But when at buck and doe
> A box of bullets I throw
> I can't hit the side of a wheelbarrow."

*   *   *   *   *

Today O'Connor joined the bunch
That stays outdoors for lunch
He says, "The deer are not nearby
And I think I smell raisin pie
So I am going to camp on that hunch."

Dimock sounded the three lakes through the ice today. The first lake by the Bubbling Spring was 21 feet plus five feet of mud. The second and third lake are both nine feet.

November 28th, 1918

Thanksgiving. About eight inches of snow and still snowing.

Everyone in this evening and no deer.

Mr. True followed a buck for three miles and the buck is still going.

Frank Munroe shot seven times at a buck, but no luck.

November 29th, 1918

McGill, Day, Davis and Hill are the only ones left in camp. Smith, Munroe, O'Connor and True left in the morning.

McGill and Day went to the old Beaver dam in the Lone Pine Country; taking their dinner in the woods. They returned with Mac's doe.

Davis and Hill hunted the swamp east of High Bridge Green. Hill had three shots. Missed.

Mac seeded the land around camp with clover in the evening.

Teamster Evans arrived at camp to haul out deer in the morning. Although we totaled only five deer, it has been one of the most delightful outings that Bucks Club has had.

Heard in camp:

"Shot them in the eyes." —O'Connor

"A cat couldn't scratch it." —Davis

"Pass the cakes." —Williams

"Roll out you!" —Herm

November 30th, 1918

Goodbye until next season.

1919

January 26th, 1919

Hello, here we are again.

   Elmer Hill, L.E. McGill and G.H. Williams drove the old
Chalmers to the Weirgor and walked in. No snow to speak of at
Ladysmith and 4 or 5 inches here in the wood except the south
slopes which are bare. Sun is shining all day and is hot; snow
melting fast. Had dinner—leaving camp at 4 P.M.

July 24th, 1919

L.E. and Allan McGill drove to Goins and took the balance on
hoof. Arrived at 7:30, each with a pack sack full of grub. About
15 pounds of it the Old Scout cooked for supper.

   The cabin was found after considerable search in the high
weeds and jungle growth in a good state of preservation, except
that much plaster had fallen.

   On our way in the dog attacked a "Porky" and was in a
pitiable condition. Thanks to some good Buck we found a pair
of pincers in the tool box and extracted more than 100 quills
and left many till the morrow. Men and dogs were tired out
with the tussle.

In order to "air out" we let in more mosquitoes than air and didn't get to sleep till about 2 A.M.

July 25th, 1919

After a good breakfast and a little later a lunch-having pulled more quills, we went to Beaver Dam. In order that the beavers might keep up their reputation of being "good workers" we tore out big gaps in the dam and then waited long for them to begin repairs, but "nothing doing."

July 26th, 1919

There may be some place hotter than this day and we may find it too, but don't believe it.

However we are determined to know more about beavers and particularly just how much repair work they can do in one night, and to see them work if possible.

Well, they made all the repairs necessary to stop the water. How they must have worked!! And we didn't see them either until this evening. So we tore out another big gap in their dam. Later in the evening we spent 1½ hours with the beavers and saw them at work at last!

November 19th, 1919

Arrived in camp and found things in bad shape. All the dishes were stolen and the door left open. Sky light broken off.

November 20th, 1919

W.A. Blackburn, Elmer Hill, O.J. Falge, H.W. True, L.C. Streater, Henry Davis, F.E. Munroe, Herm Munroe, John Yetter, Doc Day, L.E. McGill and J.W. Carow arrived in camp about 1 P.M. Found Herman Le Blanc with everything ready and a good dinner waiting.

The vandal that broke into camp had also shot a couple of holes in Tainter's fiddle. He might have escaped if he had not monkeyed with the fiddle. That was fatal, for Tainter will surely avenge that. I feel sorry for the poor duck who did it.

The weather was fine today. The snow is nearly all gone. The lake has four inches of ice. There are many tracks, but none seem fresh. It does not look like good hunting. There are many hunters around, but not so much shooting the first day.

November 21st, 1919

It drizzled all night and oozed water all day. Very low visibility. Wind from west.

Streater got a nice buck on west side of High Bridge. In P.M. Blackburn, F. E. Munroe and Alex Le Blanc drove east of High Bridge to Dimock's Knob. Falge, Elmer and Carow took stand on the Knob.

Blackburn jumped one just off the right-of-way and hurried her east with five shots. She took the trail south of the Knob and Elmer and Carow shared honors in bringing her down. We hauled her in at once.

Then we drove High Bridge Green and Elmer and Falge had shooting at another. She ran back through the Green and Streater had some fun with her. But she kept on going with her tail up.

Frank Doyle got in camp about 7 P.M. soaking wet. This is his first trip to camp and he did a good job finding us at all. Streater loaned him a pair of shirts and he looks like Charlie Chaplin in them.

November 22, 1919

Day clear with strong west wind.

We drove the Twin Greens, but the two deer we dislodged eluded us.

Doc Day got a doe near the new road about High Bridge Green. Eight deer seen today and one fox.

November 23, 1919

Day clear–strong west wind.

F.E. Munroe got a spike buck a little way from where Doc got his doe. That makes three deer this year in the same territory.

Henry Davis caught a badger in a trap on Tainter's Trail.

Billy Blackburn got a shot at a buck this P.M. He certainly can see 'em. Mr. True also got a shot at a buck. He got hair, but no buck.

November 24th, 1919

Cloudy and dark. Wind in northeast. Snowed off and on all day.

No deer killed and very few seen.

Doyle saw a doe on the long slope and got two shots at her, but never touched her. He was very cool, but could not see his sights!

Doyle and Carow went over to the Hemlock on the "Boulevard". Doyle says he can drive his Ford over it except for two ravines, and those he can jump with a good run.

It is reported that the men camped on the Hemlock saw a white deer the other day.

November 25th, 1919

Day broke very cold with strong wind from the north and northeast.

Streater and Davis fixed the skylight which had been broken open by the vandals last summer. It was interesting to hear them quarrel over it. Streater would kick about Henry's nose being in the way and Henry would stumble all over Streater's feet.

John Yetter got a doe between the first and second lakes. He and Herm hauled it in and John went back to meditate on it. A buck came along and he got that one too. While he was cleaning the buck, another one came along and nearly nosed him off the trail.

McGill wounded a buck on Tainter Trail south of the flowage but lost him. Elmer got five shots at a buck north of Twin Greens. Falge also got four shots at a doe.

Doc O'Connor arrived about 6 P.M. with news and papers that tomorrow he is going to hit them in the "opposite eye."

November 26th, 1919

Cold, but not so much wind as yesterday. Good day for hunting.

True was sick last night and did not get up in the morning.

O'Connor and Blackburn left early for the Big Ravine. Blackburn got cold and was more interested in a fire than hunting, so coming back to camp he drove two deer almost over F.E. Munroe who was caught surprised and did not get a shot. Then Blackburn drove a spike buck over to Herm Munroe, so Herm civilized him.

Streater and Davis heard the fellows driving east of the High Bridge, so they took off toward the Knob. Streater kicked a nice buck out of the swamp and shot four times at him, but he was too fast a traveler. As Davis says, he "didn't know they could run so crooked."

Falge, Blackburn and Carow went out at noon. The rest of the Bucks followed shortly thereafter, bringing an end to the 1919 deer season.

1920

April 30th, May 1st, and 2nd, 1920

Elmer W. Hill and Glenn H. Williams.

Camp in good shape—No visitors since last fall.

November 7th, 1920

L.C. Streater, Elmer Hill and G.H. Williams spent part of day at camp. Bird hunters had been in and left it dirty.

November 20, 1920

Arrivals at 12 o'clock noon: L.E. McGill, Elmer Hill, Henry Davis and Williams. P.H. McGowan of Ladysmith stopped for dinner.

Arrivals at 1 P.M.: O.J. Falge, F.M. Doyle, Carow.

Arrivals at 4:20 P.M.: H.W. True in his Ford drove to the camp door and unloaded. First car to be driven to Bucks Camp. With him as auxiliary power were Herman Munroe and Doc O'Connor.

Arrivals at 4:45 P.M.: L.C. Streater, G.W. Kase, W.A. Blackburn, F.E. Munroe. Streater drove his Overland to the foot of the hill at the High Bridge Green.

Chief Mason McGill with Patrick and Doyle carrying mud

sealed up the cracks in the outer wall. Hill and Williams put up the extra chimney and wired it. The others cut trails.

During the evening the usual smear game resumed with True as Banker.

Started raining during the evening and more or less kept it up all night.

November 21st, 1920

Le Blanc got us up at 5:30 A.M. for pancakes. Everybody sat down just as though they were real hunters and the pancakes disappeared. Then most of the bunch calmly received the report of some hardy soul that the day outside was a little unpleasant and decided not to venture out into the inclement weather but got their exercise playing smear.

Mac and Doc Day went out as usual prepared to make a day out of it—and they did, coming back at dark wet as any other rat.

It was the wettest day known here. Rained, snowed and sleeted off and on all day. What hunting that was done was of no avail. Mac and Doc wounded a buck on the Tainter Trail and then chased it back to below Tainter's where they lost it at the creek. They came across a boy with a gun. He told them the buck had passed him "seven minutes before all humped up" and that if he had known that the buck was wounded he would have killed it for them!! How's that for assininity or buck fever or something.

Not many camps near us this year, but the strangers hunted all around our camp today.

There is a big beaver house near the southwest corner of the lake. The country has had very, very little water, but the lake seems up to its old level.

November 22, 1920

These short tailed Bucks are a suspicious bunch. If this Log wasn't written in every night they imagine that they will suffer the punishment of poor hunting when they cross over Jordan.

This is the year of the "One Buck Law." Length of horn must be four inches. Diligent search was made, reports and confessions received from which it appears that no Buck in Camp can qualify except Davis. On account of this superior qualification he is becoming very disagreeable. A secret conference has decided that he must be dehorned.

O'Connor still talks about "shooting them in the eye," but stays in camp nursing an infected wrist and eating more than half the crew.

Blackburn and Doyle left yesterday and it is reported that Billy will return when he gets a change of underwear.

Streater was following a trail for several hours today before he decided that he had been trailing a snow snake instead of a buck and came back.

Deer are reported plentiful—five miles away. None were seen today.

Day traveled so far yesterday that his red pants burnt his legs and (expletive) and he is keeping quiet tonight.

> Davis, Davis, sixty years old today!
> May he live another hundred
> For we all enjoy his play
> Young in body, mind and spirit
> Shedding sunshine all the way
> A friend of sterling worth and merit
> May he never pass away.

November 23rd, 1920

Warmer this morning.

Everyone out hunting, even the invalid Doc O'Connor.

True made his annual trip to Tainter's. Examined the dam and looked over the country. He got three shots at a nice buck, but didn't connect. He was the only person to see a buck today.

Streater, Davis and Kase quit hunting deer and started hunting porcupines. Killed two in Twin Greens. Davis also scared out a Rick Lake hunter over in the Big Ravine.

Just before supper, F. Kase, Davis and Williams sounded the lake at camp and found the depths to vary from 16 to 30 feet. They took eight soundings.

The smear game didn't start very early this evening. The boys were discussing fishing, stocking lakes, etc.

November 24th, 1920

No deer killed today.

November 25th, 1920

This has been a fine day and everyone is feeling fine although no deer have been killed. Reported in log yesterday that "no deer have been killed," but Mr. True hung up a fine prong horn buck, the first to be killed. True is a foxy Buck himself—lots of action and no talk.

Herm Munroe and H.W. True trailed a bear from near the cabin to south of Tainter's and elsewhere around the country. They were both tired out and took turns kicking each other home.

Dr. O'Connor is suffering from an infected right arm which is quite serious and has confined him to the cabin since he arrived—four days now.

Williams and Hill report seeing some snow bird tracks behind the cabin. Tomorrow they are going to hunt the east end of Buck's Lake for wild turkey.

Our good cook, Herman, worked all day making a hay wire harness for Kase who will haul in camp meat and incidentally any stray buck that may be killed.

Frank Munroe got his mustache tangled in the briar brush near the Lake of the Woods and lost part of it. The other part he has consented to have trimmed.

Falge is star performer on the Victrola. He says that if his shirt tail was wet it would be just like amusing the babies at home.

If someone doesn't get a buck tomorrow Streater says there will be no Thanksgiving. And that is good gospel.

November 26th, 1920–Thanksgiving Day

Cloudy and slightly misty. No sunshine today.

Doyle came in for dinner with several hunting rumors, as usual. One was a report that Lewis Soyle, game warden, was shot while hunting north of Ingram. Another report flying around that someone at Bucks camp was shot through the neck.

Frank Munroe went out to the flowage to meet True and help him start his buck toward home. Later Davis and Streater came along and gave a hand. They were joined by Falge, Carow and Hill, making short work of it. Davis and Munroe swamped out a road until they got onto the spring trail.

The only buck shot is now reposing in the back end of the Ford car outside the camp door.

Doc O'Connor's arm is still sore, but he decided to go out with Kase, Falge and Doyle. Elmer got three shots at a buck, but too much brush.

November 27th, 1920

Still cloudy, slightly colder, no sun.

Everyone out early and feeling good. Usual crowd came back for dinner–buckless.

True came in with a tale of woe about the buck that got away after trailing him across the High Bridge Green and over the Dimock's Knob and all across the wintry north. He also reports that if there is no snow tonight he is going to do something he has never done before. And that is to take the back track of a bear. Good Luck.

Davis says some mention ought to be made of the Bloody Five—namely: Williams, Hill, Davis, Kase and Streater—just mention, neither honorable nor dishonorable.

After supper it was voted by the camp that henceforth the lake by camp be known as Bucks Lake. It was further opined that the three lakes be known as Spice Lake, Lake O'Fright and Third Lake. The hill west of Third Lake is hereby dubbed Witness Hill.

November 28th, 1920

Dark, cloudy.

Weather is getting on the nerves and if it doesn't brighten up, camp will break soon. No deer today.

November 29th, 1920

The 1920 hunting season is over.

True started out with his Ford and luggage accompanied by the Munroe brothers. Streater, Williams, Hill, Carow and Davis decided to start out in the Overland. The rest of the Bucks left shortly thereafter.

Remembrance of 1920
(Contributed by McGill otherwise known as Stump Fire Ranger)
Written in camp on December 13th, 1920

Hunters five went out for game
None of whom it is well to name
They looked about and saw an animal gray
But of sex or species none would say
Five bold hunters then stood at bay
And shot and shot with intent to stay
Some others were near of timid mein
Who turned their backs on the bloody scene
And strode far back to the friendly wood
And slyly looked back from where they stood
The bloody five with senses alert
Each proved himself a fine expert
And rolled it over on Nature's shawl
And searched in vain for a pair of balls
Then hurriedly they gazed along the range
As they saw the form of a hunter strange
And their souls within began to quail
As he came toward them on the trail
"A warden a warden," said a husky voice

"The brush for us is our only choice"
Then old grizzly with the twisted bill
Shot like an arrow up the hill
While he with stature long and wide
Sprinted with him side by side
The stranger passed as strangers will
Without a thought of grizzly or bill
Then from hillside, brush and bramble
Five sheepish bucks began to scramble
Each looked at the other with a sickly grin
And muttered something about the others sin
But insisted "grizzly" with a knowing wag
Excuse me, my pants begin to sag
Then over the hills bold and bare
Five bold hunters dragged the little Hare.

1921

April 30th, May 1st, May 2nd, 1921

Elmer Hill. L.C. Streater and G.H. Williams spent three days in camp. Found camp had been occupied by hogs during the winter. Took a trip out the West Trail and to the Big Spring. Took some pictures. Streater planted 6 balsams in front of camp brought from Bubbling Spring locality.

October 4th, 1921

L.C. Streater, Fern Streater, Elmer Hill and Mabel Hill came up for partridge season and stayed overnight. Killed six birds and had a partridge fry. Fine weather. Not many birds.

October 18th, 1921

Elmer Hill and G.H. Williams spent one night in one of the Tainter log buildings. Elmer drove his Dort to the door.

October 23rd, 1921

L.E. McGill visited this beloved hut alone. The sweet odor of skunks was present. Built a fire and ate his lunch at the spring. Saw several partridges and two rabbits.

November 11th, 1921

Cook Herman Le Blanc Jr., his brother Alex and teamster Ed Essaw arrived in camp before noon with supplies.

November 12th, 1921

L.E. McGill, Henry David, Elmer Hill and Glenn Williams arrived at camp for dinner.

P.M. F.M. Munroe, G.H. Munroe, Ed Timm, Rinold Timm, John Yetter, Max Aberhardt, S.E. McGill, E.W. Day, J.W. Carow, W.A. Blackburn, O.J. Falge, L.C. Streater reported for supper.

November 13th, 1921

Dr. O'Connor got in for dinner, brought by F.M. Doyle, accompanied by R.J. Reardon, reporter for Journal.

Two Bucks, the lucky fellows, were W.A. Blackburn and Ed Timm. Max wounded one which was picked up by some parties camped over by Tainters. Two men from Cameron were lost and directed by us.

November 14th, 1921

No bucks. Two other lost hunters arrived at 9 P.M. and were directed right way to meadow.

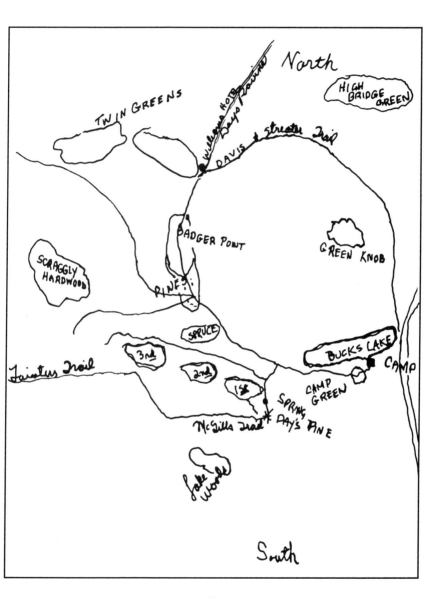

North

TWIN GREENS

HIGH BRIDGE GREEN

Williams Rob

Davis Trail

DAVIS & streater Trail

BADGER Point

GREEN KNOB

SCRAGGLY HARDWOOD

PINE?

SPRUCE

BUCKS LAKE

CAMP

Painters Trail

3rd

2nd

1st

Spring

CAMP GREEN

McGills Trail

DAY'S PINE

Lake Woods

South

November 15th, 1921

Heavy snow storm almost all day. Hunting almost impossible. McGill, Day and Streater sighted timber wolves south of Tainter's deer lick.

November 16th, 1921

F.E. Munroe gets old grand-daddy buck, a dandy five-pointed buck killed almost on Davis Stump of "Poise Hill." The Timm boys and Yetter got a nice buck near Spruce Swamp west of Dimock's Knob. Davis and Streater laid out the highway toward Twin Greens and spent the afternoon cutting it out. Light snow.

November 17th, 1921

Bad weather, more snow and wind from northeast. Poor day for hunting. Even McGill and Day slow to get out. Davis and Streater finished their trail and met Williams and Hill in the deep ravine at Twin Greens; had lunch. No deer were seen or shot at. Blackburn and Falge left after dinner for Exland to get train home.

November 18th, 1921

Snow began to fall at breakfast—another poor day for hunting. Davis, O'Connor, F.E. Munroe and Streater stayed in camp.

Others came early for dinner. McGill alone defied the elements and took his customary lunch.

Max and Ed Timm report signs of life near "Poise Hill." Some of the boys are going over after dinner settles and investigate. Everyone out after dinner mostly in East Country. No one got shooting excepting R. Timm, who did not connect. Yetter, Carow and others trailed the Buck, did not get a further glimpse.

Davis and Streater visited at "Poise Stump," blazed it, registered and came home. In the evening Streater read all thru the log to locate the year the stump was named, but it was not recorded, mention being made of it in 1917 season. It was decided after considerable conversation that it was in 1916— "Time verily does Fly."

During the evening the geography of the country was thrashed out and the creeks located. Cook offered to bet two dollars that the Weirgor Creek did not flow thru Exland. Williams located an old familiar stump with his initials on of several years ago while traveling over the new D and S trail.

November 19th, 1921

Coldest day of the season and one of the coldest in years at camp.

All hunted north. Day and McGill went north on right of way about 3½ miles and hunted west. Many signs, but no one saw a deer.

About 150 wild geese were seen.

Fred Kase came at 5:30 P.M. Smear and Penny Anty furnished a good evening's entertainment. O'Connor and Davis took the 'kale'. Doc held four fours against Davis and Timm who each held a flush.

Three inches of snow fell.

November 20th, 1921

Snow and more snow frightened such timid souls as Davis, Hill, O'Connor and Williams and they took the trail for home like a bunch of frightened coyotes after leaving orders for a car to come on the 22nd. They left at least one old Buck in the weeds comfortably housed in Storm Stump not withstanding their stampede.

Snowed all day and about noon a real blizzard from the NE was in full bloom. Snow about a foot deep and still falling at night.

Munroe and Day and Kase also left with the herd, but the report is that they were unable to keep up with the others who ran here and there on the trail and off crying "I want to get home."

However, we have a fun bunch left—Yetter, Timm, Carow, McGill and Herman.

November 21st, 1921

"The last of the Mohicans" still hunt but with less speed than usual as the snow is nearly up to the second joint above the ankle of the average Buck.

Yetter got his trap from Badger Point. Timm and Carow hunted High Bridge and Twin Greens and saw several fresh tracks. McGill hunted rabbits on his SE trail and killed four. Also reported that two bucks and three dogs crossed south of Day's Pine.

Good supper and Penny Anty, in which Bro. George took several hands and some money—novice fashion—finished a pleasant day altho a cold one.

November 22, 1921

The very last day—Carow, Timm and Yetter left camp at 8 A.M. expecting to meet auto at Meadow Dam but had to hike to Goins. McGill stayed at camp and came out with the team and supplies to LeBlanc's where auto truck was waiting to take supplies home where he arrived at 6 P.M. Thanks, Leo for sending Mac your sheepskin coat. He would have needed a wintergreen oil bath without it.

Here is hoping that all Bucks return via the same runway another year and that each kills a buck bigger than Munroe's— A MOOSE!

1922

D*uring the 1922 season, the Bucks, for some reason, made only two entries in the Log. According to the historical date following, it was during that year that they decided it was necessary to move to a different cabin in the same territory.*

Included is a poem entitled "Bucks Day" by L.E. McGill under the pseudonym "Stump Fire Ranger." Herein is captured the spirit of Bucks Camp, with eloquent and humorous references to individual members, many of which the reader may now recognize.

November 12, 1922

First arrivals in camp J.W. Carow and F.E. Munroe who found the cook, Herman Le Blanc, his brother Alex Le Blanc and teamster Floyd Graves.

Bucks arrived during the day as follows: L.E. McGill, Arthur McGill of Waupaca, E.W. Day, Elmer W. Hill, Harry Ballou, G.H. Williams, W.F. O'Connor, Geo. E. O'Connor of Eagle River, L.E. Streater, H.W. True, O.J. Falge and R.B. McDonald.

Spent the afternoon banking up the camp and mudding the cracks, setting up new heater stove, setting up and adjusting the radio set, etc. Graves left for home with his team. Sixteen men in camp first night. Bucks made up and after supper the usual smear game resumed. H.W.T. presiding.

Everyone confident of getting a buck tomorrow.

November 13th, 1922

Everybody up early and out about daylight. Harry Ballou says the reason he ate 14 pancakes for breakfast is because Carow had him up a tree for an hour yesterday stringing the radio aerial.

No deer.

BUCK'S DAY

Opening day has a magic sound,
For Twenty Bucks as they gather round,
Each has filled some mulish packs
And still another with things he lacks.

With thot of woods he doffs his grouch,
To take the trail with funny slouch.
Even the puzzle man of auburn hue
Smothers a smile when he says adieu.

Lawyers four with friendly acclaim
Agree their clients are all to blame.
That anyone who would either employ
Would every pleasure in life destroy.

A doctor smooth and not unskilled
Forgets the many graves he has filled.
Talks of his gun and what he will do
To twenty cakes and a kettle of stew.

Bankers fair, a broad even pair,
Always willing to do their share
At eating, driving or making trail
Are color decked like a parrot's tail.

A dentist puts down his only crown
And a string of plates without a frown.
Then takes his gun and looks around
And toddles off like a beegle hound.

A judge and a broker—long and short
Would steal, if they could, a little Dort.
And ride the trail in cushioned car
Trample on dignity and ethics bar.

Then came he with the twisted horn
With nothing else himself to adorn,
But actions devilish and uniform
And 60 winters since he was born.

Bright red without and green within
Came a stubby buck with a little grin,
His woodcraft he bought in a paper sack,
And carried shot for bullets on his back.

Here comes old sleepy just from his bed
With hair on his lip and none on his head.
How he kept one on and wore one away
Was in public service with little pay.

Some Bucks slumber and are ever slow,
Chewing their hash when it's time to go.
Pray ye well for a slow Buck's soul
For hell will be hot at the final goal.

The leader of all is a big boss Buck,
With no more hair than a peanut shuck.
His voice is heard in the morning fog
"Attention all and hide your grog!"

"A Buck has wandered far, far away
To that golden shore and a holiday.
Just for a moment cease your fun
To send him greetings on the rising sun."

"Now go to the hills and rippling spring,
Listen to the voice of the Wolf dog's ring!
To beaver's splash and the snort of deer,
Commune with cosmos and the gods of cheer."

Bucks keep a log in which is writ
A bit of truth and a little wit.
Now, old Buck, should you log this down,
Remember about "kickin that hown dog round!"

       Stump Fire Ranger

1923

November 10, 1923

The cabin we now occupy was one of a number built 45 years ago by the Knapp-Stout Co. who occupied same for some 15 years after which they were looked after by D.L. Tainter until his death by suicide in Nov. 1917. After that they were used only by wandering hunters until they became uninhabitable.

On June 1st, L.E. and A.R. McGill came here to examine the cabin with the intention of making repairs. They came again June 23rd and A.R. stayed on the job and rebuilt and made numerous alterations and repairs which he completed about Nov. 10th.

His "side kicker" L.E. made 10 trips here during the summer. Other Bucks came and we have enjoyed the fishing and bird and duck hunting more than ever before.

The house, a picture of which is in the front of this Log, was occupied by Tainter for about 30 years and was burned by parties unknown in the spring of 1920 together with several other buildings. It was a pretty home with beautiful trees, shrubs, and grounds—an oasis in a desert of waste.

Adorning our cabin are several relics of the days when logging was done with oxen. The cabin it will be observed is unique in structure. Lumbermen and "Jacks" of this generation never

before saw such roof construction, which indicates at least that pine had little value half a century ago. But who cares for the past? We have a Victrola, and jazz sounds much sweeter—more "peppy," you know, than musty tales of the past.

November 11th, 1923

Harry Ballou, Dr. E.W. Day and J.W. Carow came to camp via "Meadow Dam." Lunched at the old cabin and got here at 4:00 P.M. Arthur served supper and all were well filled but Harry—his capacity is yet our unknown quantity—cooks can't do it!

Henry Davis came with John Diamond, County Surveyor, on Thursday the 8th to survey our lines. We found him two miles south of camp blazing a circle-like trail—said in explanation, he was trying to follow his nose to camp.

November 12th, 1923

G.H. Williams, O.J. Falge, Elmer H. Hill and R.B. McDonald and Herman Le Blanc came. Four mighty hunters and a cook all in one day very much awed the first comers. So much so that Davis took to the woods. McGill took something else and Harry took two meals in one.

We visited Pickeral Lake. The past two days were warm—yesterday hot. The whole country is very dry. Forest fires burned over nearly all territory except north of the Flowage and east of our "Woods Road" where there should be good hunting. Tonight there was some rain.

November 13th, 1923

Arrivals: L.E. Streater and F. Munroe. Both took kindly to the woods and saw "meat." Frank insisted east was west but finally yielded to the persuasive Streater who insisted that his compass was shooting straight. It beats all how a man loses his mind when he gets a U.S. job.

Eleven deer were seen—one killed. Harry swears the one he saw was flying. Last year he flew when he saw a bear, and other things happened, too.

The Fan Tan game is in full bloom. Mac D's "O Soul of Mine" has driven Davis insane. He hasn't much knowledge of souls 'no how!

Raining this eve and warm.

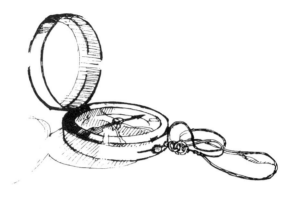

November 14th, 1923

Ladies Day!! Yes, Mrs. Ballou and Mrs. Day, the first women to come to camp during the deer season paid us a visit driving with Thos. Bordman who stayed to hunt.

Ballou and Falge and Mac Donald left after dinner and John Yetter and Max Eberhardt came in by auto from Wisconsin Rapids.

Warm day—a little rain. No sun since the season opened.

No deer have been seen but signs plentiful.

November 15th, 1923

Nice day to hunt and still warm. The Bucks wandered far over the country and all are happy. Some of them began to look stuffed from eating so much. I can't say "over eating" for it is impossible to fill one of them.

There was a young man named Carow
Who drove a big Pierce Arrow
While out in the fog, he ran over a dog
Honk, honk, Baloney.

November 16, 1923

As Pat Wilson would say "Nutin stirin." Bordman says tomorrow he is going to walk backwards to keep the deer from eating his lunch.

Streater and Davis continue to explore and survey imaginary lines. Williams and Hill are sore about losing their job.

Day and the McGills found the CR and N down at H. P. Lake and many miles of trail—nothing more.

Some colder—NW wind but not freezing.

November 17th, 1923

The following left today: John Yetter, Max Eberhardt, Henry Davis and L.C. Streater.

This A.M. at 7, we drove thru along the river. The only deer broke thru the lines and went west. Then we all went to Pickeral Lake where Day and the McGills left the others going N.E. Several deer were seen. Day and the McGills had shooting.

Search was made for a bee tree after Hill explained how easy it was to find one. Here is the way it is done: get a good stout stick and pound on a tree; if you are stung it is a bee tree.

Carow told stories of spirits and spooks until Herman could see them too—the real thing.

This was the first bright day of the season—warm and delightful in the 'big wood.'

BUCKS CAMP PHOTO ALBUM

The big beaver house, 1928

Crossing the flowage.

Bird Hunting, 1917

Spring visit, 1921

Bucks Camp

Four loyal Bucks and the original Log

There's Le Blanc from Quebec,
Who fell in the lake to his neck,
When we asked, "Are you friz?"
He replied, "Yes I is",
"But we don't call this cold in Quebec."

"Now it's
venison"

There's Bill with the hairy chin,
Who is so exceedingly thin,
That when he essayed,
To drink lemonade,
He slipped thru the straw and fell in.

The Spirit of Jack.

A Lumber Jack slept in a bed of straw,
And dreamed of how he would practice law.
Of how he slept and how he dined,
Drank the corn juice and the wine.

Of Jacks, a good sort of their kind,
Rough made in manner, heart and mind;
To trail them in the coming years
Would only dim my eyes with tears.

To keep on felling the lofty pine,
To spend my all, my every dime
On women, wine and jazzy song,
Needs no Saint to say its wrong.

Young I am and bad my way
For I am only common clay,
But I can rise above this pall
And be a man in spite of all.

I have no friends to pave the way,
No guiding hand to a better day;
Except that little thing called "will"
That all creation cannot kill.

This I'll hitch to some fixed star
To direct me to another bar;
To where, according to the code,
Naught but justice hath abode.

Jacks can fight and never sign,
Fight if need be until they die.
I'll take their spirit and naught confess,
May the God of Fortune each one bless.

Four o'clock brought the ringing call,
"Roll out you terriers one and all"!
Jack sat up and his mind was keen
To make his life just like the dream.

For many years he used ax and saw,
From borrowed books he got some law.
He found a friend, a gallant knight
Who rose like Thor to help him fight.

A friend is only true blue made,
By standing straight and unafraid.
A jewel then of rich design,
Superb in luster, in worth sublime.

So with many tools and pluck,
He mixed sunshine with his luck;
Just as any smiling Jack might do
Who loved the sport of going through.

"Maritial relations" were all too slow,
The Rule in Shelly's an awful blow.
So he put them together as law and fact
And turned them over and turned them back.

His anchor held and he reached the goal,
But found no sign of the Jacks of old,
No Capsan, Boom, nor pine tree raft,
No song or story of the ancient craft.

But there in a chair like a falcon, old,
Sat he whose blood for years was cold.
Twelve disciples with opinions rank
Sat in places with faces blank.

The Jack looked over this cold array,
Thought of the sunshine on Catfish Bay;
Of Lake and stream, of secluded nook,
And turned away with a sheep skin book .

J. E. McGill

Two bobcats and three good bucks.

Flambeau River, 1926

Joe Cundy's big fish

The Bucks

The Bucks & Sons

"Stump Fire Ranger"

Elmer Hills
Bear

G. H. Williams

F. E. Munroe

1924

November 9th, 1924

The McGills arrived early to avoid Big Buck McCorrson and his carload of assets. A.R., Geo. and L.E. reached camp at dark. Warm day—snow about gone but some frost still on the ground.

November 10th, 1924

A.R. went to Birchwood to get meat and balance of supplies, also to see Zollabach about wood for camp.

Geo. and I cut wood all the forenoon—stumps and anything we could find and carry in. Our efforts netted about 1½ cords.

Some years ago I would and did refuse to cut wood. But age is reducing me to a state of "non compos mentis" and fools are happy.

George saw two deer—the first wild ones he ever saw. We didn't take our guns into the woods. We did fix stove pipes etc.

November 11th, 1924

Rained last night and all this A.M. During the P.M., A.R. and Geo. went to the Burned Bridge and I went SE 2½ miles on Sorenson's Trail where I ate lunch; then I cut trail west and north all afternoon.

The first named saw two deer and I saw two. No one carried guns. There were some shots fired south west but none elsewhere.

Sorenson saw several—including two bucks—within the past week. One of them looked like a moose, he said.

November 12th, 1924

3:30 P.M. McCorrison, Ballou, Day, Williams and the cook Le Blanc arrived in McGill's limousine.

4:30 P.M. Frank Munroe, Herm Munroe and Max Eberhardt arrived in Max's car.

Sorrenson and his brother-in-law are over at the east camp for a few days to discourage hunters locating there.

November 13th, 1924

Breakfast at 6:30. All out by 7:00.

Camp meat located and hung up by 8:00.

Max located and killed a black bear about a mile south of camp. Shot him twice thru the head and once thru the body. When we went back after lunch, it was still breathing. Dressed and hung him up.

Geo. McGill got a nice buck on Lawless Creek.

Doc O'Connor and W.E. Thompson rolled into camp abut 4.

12 hunters and one cook in camp.

Wet snow and wind.

November 14th, 1924

Clear and fine. Tracking snow, no deer.

November 15th, 1924

Max got two nice bucks on the logging road toward Lawless Creek. Geo. (A.R.) McGill got another buck north.

November 16th, 1924

Herm Munroe, Max and Harry Ballou with two bucks and bear left for Wis. Rapids (Ballou to Ladysmith). Streater and Elmer

Hill arrived at noon. O'Connor and Thompson left for home at 4:30.

November 17th, 1924

All out hunting. No results.

November 18th, 1924

Day registered with one nice buck. Bear track followed by L.E. McGill and Sorrenson.

November 19th, 1924

Sorrenson took up the bear track at 6 and followed it down a mile west of Sternbergs and up Devils Creek and quit at noon and came home. L.E. Mac got a nice buck across the flowage.

November 20th, 1924

Breakfast at 6. All out in the woods early and hunted until noon. Dinner at 11. Packed up and started home—Streater, L.E. McGill, A.R. McGill, Munroe, Hill, Day, and Williams and Le Blanc in two cars.

1925

The year 1925 marked the first closed deer hunting season in Wisconsin. This was the beginning of alternate annual closed and open seasons as established by the Legislature after responding to petitions from the deer counties.

If the members of Bucks Camp were particularly upset with this state of affairs, they did not record their feelings in the Log. Instead, they contented themselves through the year with fishing, grouse hunting and camp activities.

June 1st, 1925

L.E. McGill and C.A.S. fished in Bucks Lake. Caught 6 crappies and 52 bluegills.

June 4th, 1925

H.F. Davis and C.A. went trout fishing. Got back about 10 o'clock with 40 trout. Caught a couple pike on the pond in the afternoon.

July 5th, 1925

Mac, Davis and C.A. went fishing in Bucks Lake. Caught 18 bass weighing from ½ to about 3 pounds. Returned to the water all but one which we had for supper.

July 22nd, 1925

> "So This Is Bucks"
> We ne'er had hoped to land in this,
> The famed camp of Utopian bliss,
> But since we now all quite agree,
> With what we've heard from J.W.C.,
> We wish in your Log the thanks to inscribe,
> Of several more of the "Carow" tribe.
>
> The Carow Family

Caught 28 pike and returned 12 to the water.

August 22nd, 1925

L.E. McGill and Allen came and stayed until the 25th. We caught six large pike in about an hour. Allen caught one that weighed about seven pounds. The new porch is a pleasure. Allen slept there and heard a wolf bark and a deer splashing and snorting just below the dam.

October 2, 1925

F.E. Munroe, L.E. McGill, A.R. McGill and J.L. McCorrison came at dusk via Canton. Dr. Day, G.H. Williams and Elmer W. Hill came after dark. Many birds, wild and hard to get. Weather fine. Some rain and frost.

McCorrison found the "Rock Deposit" and some other ancient stones which convinced F.E. Munroe that the earth is at least 100 years old.

The "Lake Island" floated into opening to lake and L.E.M. tried to cut thru with jack-knife. Lost knife, broke fish rod. Joe used the proper language to comfort him and they explored "Devils Lake" and called it good.

Fishing good—12 good ones in the box and as many more in the bellies of a hungry bunch. Joe caught 9 of the 12.

The crew finished two chimneys, all hands throwing "mud" and "bull" like real workmen.

Day and Mac lunched and drank at the Bubbling Spring on October 4th.

October 6th, all left after dinner.

November 6th, 1925

"Silent Joe" McCorrison and "Klondike Art" McGill delivered themselves at 2 P.M. in Art's 4 wheel vehicle. They immediately started planting the rice and showed that for once in their lives they had good judgement, for by nightfall the thermometer showed 4 below. At 7 P.M. Frank McCorrison and Harry Ballou also "ballou" in.

Joe McCorrison and Harry Ballou were not on speaking terms as neither spoke to the other more often than every 46 seconds.

November 7th, 1925

Albert Krugle of Wabeno who owns 320 acres adjoining was
found near here with a crew of surveyors. They were sleeping
here and eating at Sorenson's. They are locating their lines
which in turn is aiding us in finding our lines.

The weather was fine—clear and snappy. Ice on the pond
nearly strong enough to hold us up. No snow.

No runs—no hits—no errors.

November 13, 1925

J.L. McCorrison, A.R. McGill, L.E. McGill met here without
prearrangements. Joe and A.R. came via Weyerhauser over the
"new road." In fact, now it is no road at all with the frost out.
They worked for hours to get up a hill, which they described as
hell and worse. Big language for men who profess to being
"deacons."

L.E. drove via Canton in 2 hours and 25 minutes. We explored
the woods between the new survey lines. Weather at about freezing.

Great argument between Joe and L.E. over which way to move
gun sights to change direction of bullet. Question still unsettled
even tho Sorenson consulted.

Joe also maintains that worms can and do change basswood
trees to poplars. But then he says he is just as happy as if he
knew something.

November 15th, 1925

Leaving in the P.M. A good time was had by all.

December 4th, 1925

L.E. McGill came alone—No, his Ford came with him. He stayed several days. Sixteen inches of snow fell. He walked to Birchwood and the Ford stayed behind.

It turned out that the Ford had to stay there until May 8, 1926, the date of the first visit of Bucks at camp. Before setting out on foot, however, the Stump Fire Ranger recorded the following poem in the Log. He prefaced it with: "In memory of the Bucks whom I loved, let me inscribe:"

IN MEMORIAM

The Bucks are dead; please call the hearse.

They long have been cold; it couldn't be worse.

Once they stood like strong and virile men,

But that is a story of what might have been.

They discarded their guns for lipstick red.

Why wonder then that their souls have fled?

Once they were active and together were strong.

But with powder and puff they all went wrong.

Their interest and action gave way to words,

And they twittered away like sparrow birds.

They deserted the places and things they loved well,

To follow a trail that they thought more swell.

These poor old Bucks who once held sway,

With foible and fashion they fell by the way.

Like David of old they lay without heat,

Nor all of the virgins could e'en warm their feet.

So step gently, friends, and pull the shroud,

For in Life these Bucks were very proud.

1926

May 8th, 1926

E.W. Day, A.R. and L.E. McGill came this Saturday evening in Day's car. Weather ideal and roads fine. Bacon and eggs satisfied our appetites.

We were surprised and much pleased to find our cabin beautifully decorated in white—thanks to our friends the Sorenson's. We enjoyed a most refreshing sleep in well-aired blankets. I wet nursed the Ford which has been here since last December. After two hours work I announced her as being filled and ready to be wheeled out for an airing.

Day and Sorenson are trying to puncture the Sabbath with their fish poles. I'm nicely settled down in the big, cane chair, nerves all quieted by the smell of the wild.

June 14th, 1926

The whole Day family drove up after 2 P.M. via Weyerhauser. Had our supper here and all report a fine time. There were six of us, but we only took five fish home though we could have taken more.

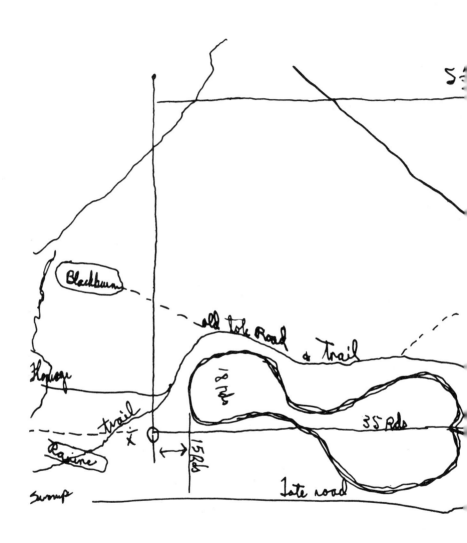

Blackburn

old tote Road & Trail

18 Rds

35 Rds

Hovaje

trail

Ravine

x

15 Rds

Swamp

Tote road

S

24

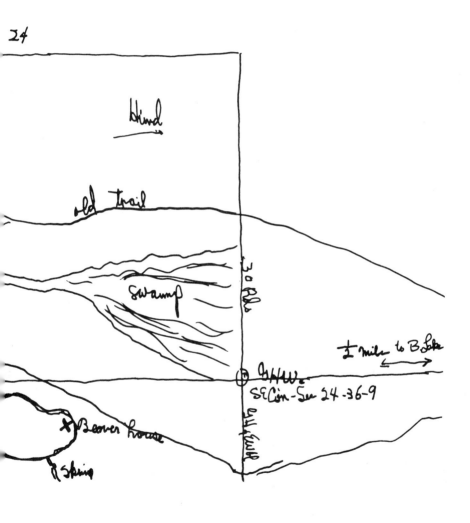

Blind

old Trail

Swamp

30 Rds

½ mile to B. Lake

S44W
SE Cor - Sec 24 -36-9

N47W

× Beaver House

Spring

July 10th, 1926

Here we are again on the job,
Wife and I without a sob.
We fish and sleep and walk and eat.
Do it all over then sit on our seat.
I cook one meal and she cooks two,
Trout and pike and a kettle of stew.
We sleep in an "upper" to be near the bats,
When I snore, I'm poked in the slats.

July 27th, 1926

Party from Wisconsin Rapids report all happy and pleased with
the place except the bats at night. Caught 18 fish all told. Many
thanks, Bucks, for a good time.

September 9th, 1926

Guests from St. Petersburg, Florida report this is the only place
they don't alibi about their fishing.

November 27th, 1926

Cold and six inches of snow found Joe McCorrison and the two
McGill's A.R. and L. E., on the way full of "hope and anticipa-

tion," as Joe said. After an all day struggle with snow and car trouble, we arrived with the help of a team from Fuca's.

November 28th, 1926

Sorenson repaired car in such a masterly manner that it held together for the trip on Monday. He can fix anything and shoot the whiskers off a woodtick by way of pastime.

A.R. sick with flu. Weather continues cold. We enjoy the camp altho all here have colds.

November 30th, 1926

F.E. Munroe, G.H. Munroe, E.W. Hill, G.H. Williams, E.W. Day, Earl Young and Dan Rosenthal came with Herm Le Blanc, the cook, just after noon—Day's car. Trouble with snow and flat tires reported.

December 1st, 1926

H.W. True, O.J. Falge, W.F. O'Connor came with True in time for supper. More snow has fallen in the past few days but no trouble in coming.

December 2nd, 1926

L.C. Streater, W.E. Thompson, Gerald and Bobbie Streater came, making in all 17 which fills all beds.

Snow falls frequently. Six inches in woods, but everyone is happy. Deer are more plentiful than at any time in 15 years. Four to 9 are seen by nearly every one each day, but nearly all does and fawns. Elmer saw 6 together and Glenn saw 10 together. Art saw 4 drilling along in "a string."

December 5th, 1926

Five inches of snow fell yesterday—knee deep in the swamps now. L.E. crawled out after dinner and killed a 4 prong. It was smaller than Joe's 180 pounder, but of course better eating. At least so he says. But Joe says he doesn't know a damned thing about venison and less about the woods.

The Munroe family and the two boys from Wisconsin Rapids left after dinner. The big snow fall alarmed them. The remainder of the crew are "hard boiled." Even Tommy with a lame hip ropes it and enjoys miles of snow plowing on the hoof. Herb True wanders around the Big Ravine, a circuit of 10 miles and wonders why his game leg gets tired. Dr. Day made a trip with Gerry around Kegema Lake. Wore the tail of his Mackinaw off and lost his lunch, but satisfied his wanderlust with 11½ miles.

A bunch went over to the Lake of the Woods to get Joe's buck. Streater insisted he was the best lead mule in those "diggin's" and that he would make trouble for any pie hunter who thot he could take the lead. Joe snorted, but fell behind and was

106

heard to ask if he would lose his title of "Mayor" if he let that big Moose nose him out.

Glenn and Elmer furnish a real sensation by taking their lunch and eating it on "Streater's Pinicle." Dr. O'C eats and sleeps and then does it again. He says we are punk hunters and that when he gets ready, he'll "shoot em in the eye."

Last night signals were shot after dark. Turned out to be Ed Planz and Gerald Hefty, cheesemakers between Campia and Mikanna who were lost on the creek near "Streater's Pinicle." They came to camp this A.M. They were 24 hours without food, had no compass and spent a cold night.

December 6, 1926

Twenty-two below zero last night, but sunshine and warmer today.

The cook left on account of his mother's illness, but our versatile "Mayor" took charge and turned out open face, closed face and bare faced pies and proved himself a master chef. We all start for home in the morning.

1927

The year 1927 was designated by the Legislature as the second closed season of alternate annual deer hunting seasons. This did not prevent the Bucks from making at least a few visits to camp. They jotted these notes and observations during summer and fall.

July 7th, 1927

Munroe and Rev. Mielecki arrived at 8 P.M. Found camp clean. Went to bed and had a good sleep. Fish for breakfast. Fish for supper. Saw another bear swim the pond.

July 22nd, 1927

L.E. and Allan. Weather hot but fine. No flies or mosquitoes—remarkable for the season of the year.

Saw deer, mink, beaver and ducks. Swimming—good. Fishing—fair. Enough to eat—none taken away. If we are to have good fishing, we had better eat our fish at camp. I just filled all 3 lamps.

Good time—sorry to leave.

October 5th, 1927

Elmer Hill, Glenn Williams, Ed Worden and O.J. Falge spent all day fishing and eating and talking—mostly talking, with Worden taking first prize. Left in the rain but had a good time.

October 14th, 1927

O'Connor and Willard Thompson hunting and supper. Caught six nice fish.

1928

May 25th, 1928

McGill and Williams, the well known firm of attorneys of
Ladysmith, Wisconsin reached camp at 2:30 P.M. Found everything in excellent condition with Alfred Sorenson and family in
charge. Spent the afternoon fishing—results slight. The senior
member of the firm cooked supper.

Left for home at 9 P.M.

August 28th, 1928

The Munroe family. Fish to eat, but not biting good. Lots of
blackberries to eat and a few bats for night performances. Helps
shorten the nights. Had a fine time.

September 8th, 1928

McGill here to check on possibility of a new road. Went with
Sorenson to look for road to the "Bubbling Spring" as far as the
"Deer Lick" and found that such a road can be made at small
cost by crossing the creek just below the dam and follow the

brow of the hill to where it connects with the toll road. This would eliminate building corduroy over the swamp and the old road is good to the "big hole" where the tornado raised hell.

Saturday I went alone from the "Deer Lick" to the "Big Spring" on the south side of the 3 lakes, and the old toll road is good to a point near the east of the end of the flowage. Here a new road could be built along the hill south of where the old one follows this low marsh. The distance is not great.

I just walked and incidentally filled my belly—excuse me—stomach, with blackberries.

September 15th, 1928

Joe McCorrison came in with his friend John Cundy of Marshfield.

After dinner Sorenson took us up to the lake to fish. They were sure biting. We caught 11 in an hour. Then Cundy had a piece of luck which is unique, but is characteristic of these waters where you may expect anything. After catching four nice fish, Cundy got on another good one which would weigh two or three pounds. While pulling it in, he was astonished to see a whopper of a fish nearly swallow it! He kept his head and kept them both coming and slid them both over the side of the boat. Then the big one let go and there was some scramble to keep the fish, especially the big one, from jumping out of the boat.

Sorenson realized at once that this was the biggest fish ever caught in these waters and, wanting to keep it alive, immediately headed the boat for camp. The fish weighed 14¾ pounds and was 38 inches long. It sure was a beauty. Joe says he is sure the guys in Marshfield will never believe the story and he would like to take Sorenson along to cram it down their throats.

In the evening several flocks of ducks flew over. The day was beautiful and the stars were out when we went to bed.

September 16th, 1928

Began to rain in the night and kept it up half the morning. The pond is very high, lots of water running over the dam. Mr. Cundy is having sport catching fish out of the pool below the dam and putting them in the pond above.

While sitting around the stove and listening to the rain the boys are having a lot of fun telling yarns as in the old days.

Joe sure does liven things up with his stories and repartee. It seems fine to have him around again.

Sun came out about noon.

Joe and Cundy went out about 1 P.M.

Doc got two coots.

We caught a few more fish so all had 3 to take out.

Before Joe and Cundy left we took pictures of the big fish with Cundy holding it.

September 18th, 1928

G.H. Williams and wife arrived at 4 P.M. and left at 4:15 P.M. Called for a drink of spring water.

September 24th, 1928

Elmer, Glenn and Sorenson went up to the pond to fish. Fish were not biting well at first. Finally, when they were thinking of coming back to camp, Elmer said, "Let's stay 10 more minutes and I'll catch one a minute." The fish actually started biting right then and Elmer made good the first four minutes, catching five fish. Then he got cold feet, quit and they came home.

Saw five deer, two partridges and a big red-headed woodpecker.

November 30th, 1928

L.E. McGill, Dr. Day and Gerald Day and Art McGill got in about 11 A.M.

F.E. Munroe and J.W. Carow with Wilmer and John Carow came in about 12:30 P.M.

Glenn Williams, Elmer Hill and Herman Le Blanc, the cook, came in at 3 P.M.

Dr. O'Connor and H.W. True got in about supper time, and long after dark Art McGill's boy and grandson got in.

Herman got the groceries put away and prepared one of his excellent meals.

The flowage was frozen and the boys put on their skates and went up the pond with J.W. inspecting the beaver and muskrat houses.

There is one beaver house in Doughnut Lake six feet tall and sixteen feet in diameter. Sorenson says it is the biggest he ever saw. The beaver have been very busy cutting popple all along the flowage. Some of the trees felled are 6 to 8 inches through. There seem to be more beaver than rats. Just above the first bend the ice has not frozen, although elsewhere it is 4 inches thick.

There are hanging in the shed 2 wildcat and one bear hide. Besides that, Sorenson has 20 raccoons. He had a wolf in a trap, but it got away.

There are campers all around us from everywhere. Must be 200 hunters in the vicinity. They are in tents and cabins of every description. There will be a great bombardment tomorrow.

December 1st, 1928

Herman got us up fairly early—5 A.M.! We were all up and raring to go long before daylight. Herman baked his famous buckwheat cakes for breakfast. The boys sure sailed into them. Wilmer Carow was heard to say, "I'll show these birds how to eat cakes." All the boys did just that.

The hunters could not wait and started out as early as they could see. The visibility was very poor and the sky was spitting snow.

The bombardment started soon after daylight. None of our boys shot a gun as no one saw a buck except Art McGill's grandson. He shot a slug at it.

Altho none of us saw a buck except this boy, the woods must be lousy with them because we heard over 150 shots before 8 A.M. These numerous foreign hunters have wonderful eyesight or else they are shooting at everything they see.

December 2nd, 1928

Still snowing slightly. Visibility very poor. Again the bombardment started with daylight and continued all day.

Dr. Day and Gerald came in with a big buck. It had been wounded by two hunters before they got it. There was a slug hole, a 30-30 bullet and some buck shot in it. Likely the buck the McGill boy shot at.

In the P.M. Carow had a hunch and went over to the canal. In about 5 minutes after he got set, some foreign hunters drove buck on to him from the south. He dropped it on the trail and brought it in. It slipped fairly easily on the snow.

Many does and fawns were seen. Everybody saw deer but only two or three bucks. No shots—only flashes in the brush.

The underground telegraph tells us the foreign hunters are killing does and taking them out at night.

One bunch of hunters had the nerve to drive their car into our backyard down the creek. Mac told them a few things they needed to know, but they stayed all day and pulled out in the P.M. They paid no attention to our "Private Property" signs.

Mac, Doc and Art are still staying out all day. The rest of us came in for pie. Herman's pies are sure alluring.

December 3rd, 1928

Glenn and Elmer went over to the old camp. Sorenson shot a buck from the pinicle west of the old camp.

Frank, Doc and J.W. hunted in the canal country. J.W. drove a buck onto a farmer who was standing on our road near Bowler Creek. This farmer had not been in the woods 20 minutes. Isn't

it hell? Frank was not 20 rods away when the farmer shot. As usual our boys hunt too far away from camp and others come into our land and get the deer.

Everybody saw does and fawns today.

The bombardment south and north died down somewhat.

Sorenson made some nice shots at the buck target near the old camp. He shot it four times. Three of the bullets can be covered with one hand. Anyone would have been fatal. The boys report the camp in good shape.

Snow was wet today and all the boys are busy greasing their leather tops.

It snowed off and on all day, visibility bad, no sun.

The Fan Tan game is on tonight. That sure is a scientific game! Herman is kicking because he gets all Aces and Kings. It's hard to satisfy some men.

December 4th, 1928

The day opened dark, cold and windy with snow blowing level from the northwest.

Mac went south as usual. Frank and Doc tried the canal; Glenn and Elmer southeast. J.W. and Sorenson went to the old camp. Mr. True to the north and east. Very little shooting today.

Many deer tracks east along the trail, one old buck track was 3 inches across; another fawn track one could cover with a nickel. The deer were milling around all night but none crossed north. Mac reports he saw 5 does; Mr. True saw 2 bucks and a doe. Elmer saw some does. Doc saw none. Sorenson was over in the Big Ravine. He left a stand to look at a trap and came back in 15 minutes. While he was gone a big buck walked across his track.

Sorenson showed us the place he caught the bear. It sure created havoc with the trees and logs. It broke off popples and birches with its paws, chewed off some, split and splintered logs and made it look as tho a small cyclone had struck. It climbed a popple 4 inches in diameter and broke off a birch 15 feet from the ground. This shows a bear can climb a small tree. It is hard to believe that a 200 pound bear can do so much damage to trees and logs.

The underground telegraph says that 26 men went in south of us this morning in one crowd. They killed 5 bucks in there yesterday. It also tells us that a bunch north killed a doe and cut out some of the meat and left the rest. Another crowd killed a doe west of our meadow and cleaned it out. They came in after it about 4 P.M., but saw one of our boys and turned around and drove off.

It turned out clear and cold. Doc predicted clear weather tomorrow and no wind. J.W. said there would be wind. We will see.

December 5th, 1928

Doc was right. It opened clear and cold today—7 below zero. J.W. was right too—a cold west wind.

Four of the boys—the fellows who stay out all day—went east in the Bubbling Spring country. J.W. Sorenson went over to the Big Ravine. Elmer and Glenn went south. Elmer had a lot of fun with a doe. She came right up to him in the creek and took a drink, then wandered off.

Glenn saw a big buck and got a shot through the brush but could not find him. He went out through the canal. Doc and Frank had been there but he dodged them.

The outsiders are still hunting our territory west.

Mr. True warmed up his car and went out.

Mac wounded a buck near Pickeral Lake and followed for an hour but had to leave it. He thinks he broke the left front leg.

Glenn got another shot at a buck in late P.M. He drew blood, could not find the deer.

December 6th, 1928

Mr. True and O.J. Falge came in about 1 A.M. Joe McCorrison and son Frank and W.E. Thompson got in just after dinner.

True brought up some live minnows and went out to try for fish. He got eight.

George McGill got a spike buck near Arpins Hardwood. Mac and Sorenson trailed Mac's wounded buck over to the right-of-way. It was still going strong when they left it.

Glenn and Elmer took up the trail of the deer Glenn wounded the day before. They followed it to where some one else had cleaned it and taken in out.

Geo. McGill got a shot at a gray fox.

Falge saw two deer before he had been in the woods a half an hour. Many deer were seen today.

This morning we were standing on the brink of the ravine, called the "canal" by our boys, and we were treated to an example of deer woodcraft which was wonderful.

Hoping to waylay an unsuspecting buck which attempted to cross, we had taken our station on the rim of this valley. After 15 minutes of waiting, we heard a twig break. We turned our heads and looked into the eyes of a doe standing alert about 200 feet away. Behind her was a little fawn. She surveyed us intently for several minutes. Finally she decided we were not dangerous but, just the same, a little more distance would be advisable. She turned and proceeded away from us a short distance; the fawn following close behind. She then turned and carefully surveyed us again. We had not moved and the wind was toward us. She was satisfied with us and now gave her attention to the perilous journey across the "valley-of-the-shadow-of-death." Before venturing, she looked carefully in every direction, tested the air with her nose and listened with her large ears erect. After a careful inspection, she twitched her tail and proceeded down the side of the ravine, the fawn standing immovable. The doe went down the slope very carefully and slowly one foot at a time; eyes, ears and nose on alert for man, the killer. Her progress was like a slow-motion picture of a thoroughbred race horse, knees high, head erect. When she reached the bottom of the ravine, at a signal we missed, the fawn came down to her. Still alert, she then started across the floor of the valley-of-the-shadow. The fawn, at a signal, joined her and together they quickly went up the side and out of sight.

It was as beautiful a piece of woodcraft as we have ever seen; careful, cautious, silent, scientific. The only mistake made was the first brush crack. Except for that we would not have seen the crossing. For a buck this error would have been fatal. During the journey we were as anxious for their safety as was the old doe. We felt ourselves mentally urge her to hurry. When the deer was gone—we hate to admit it—there was a lump in our throats, and we

wanted to call the doe and tell her that the valley-of-the-shadow was not a dangerous place, but the safest refuge in the world.

For the first time the table was full. Fifteen in camp. Herman's graham cake, like his Johnny cake, was especially good.

December 7th, 1928

Clear and cold.

All out hunting bright and early after a good feed of Herman's cakes.

By noon most of the hunters were back for dinner.

O'Connor, True and Carow packed up and left for home taking Carow's buck with them. Geo. McGill took Arthur McGill and George's buck and left.

Doc Day got a nice buck over east in the hardwood. He hauled it home. At 4 P.M. Gerald Day drove to camp. Doc loaded his buck and left for home. Gerald stayed to hunt until Sunday.

During the evening a new game took possession of the fan—a game called "Stud." The cook, who insists on being the banker, went broke.

December 8th, 1928

Clear and very cold. Also windy.

All out on the trails. Joe hauled in a buck from near the Lake of the Woods and Elmer took a shot at a flag.

Falge and Sorenson just came in dragging a buck as did also Jerry Day and Frank McCorrison.

Although the Bucks could not have forseen that the following entry was to be the very last one written in the Log, the concluding sentence could hardly have been more typical, or more fitting.

December 9th, 1928

Everybody up bright and early at the call of Herman that the buckwheat cakes (round and brown) were ready to serve. And were they ready! Delicious, appetizing and invigorating.

The sun came over warm and inviting and all were off early and in many directions.

"So step gently, friends, and pull the shroud,
For in Life these Bucks were very proud."